AT THE FOOT OF THE CROSS

Easter Dramatic Readings

Barbara Dan

WestBow Press
A Division of Thomas Nelson

WestBow Press books may be ordered through booksellers or by contacting:

WestBow Press
A Division of Thomas Nelson
1663 Liberty Drive
Bloomington, IN 47403
www.westbowpress.com
1-(866) 928-1240

ISBN: 978-1-4497-6142-4 (sc)
ISBN: 978-1-4497-6141-7 (e)

Library of Congress Control Number: 2012913698

Printed in the United States of America

WestBow Press rev. date: 08/14/2012

Twelve Easy-to-Use Dramatic Readings For the Lenten Season and Easter Week

In Jesus' day during Passover Week, Jews gathered from all over Israel to remember God's liberating power in leading His people out of bondage. People of every social class, race, and nationality came together to seek God's blessing and spiritual renewal.

This edition of Dramatic Readings captures the possible thoughts and reactions of many whose lives were deeply touched by the life and ministry of our Lord Jesus Christ.

Besides using traditional characters known to have been present during the Crucifixion, author Barbara Dan has utilized her creative skills as a screenwriter, and her knowledge of the Bible and customs at that time, to explore the strong possibility that other biblical characters may also have found their way to Jerusalem during Holy Week. Because of the crowds thronging the city, she believes that it is highly likely that many acquainted with Jesus' ministry may very well have made their way outside the city walls to observe the Crucifixion and death of our Lord Jesus Christ.

In all of these dramatic readings, the author seeks first and foremost to remain faithful to the biblical and historic records, and the transforming message of the Gospels. Each of the characters speaks from his/her spiritual need and/or moral dilemma in ways that will surely connect with today's audiences.

These sketches may be edited, shortened, or presented in a different order, in order to fit a variety of performance situations, including worship, classroom discussion, public performance in malls, theaters, schools, fairs, and open air events.

Costumes may be as simple as a head scarf, full biblical garb, or dramatic sketches may be presented in contemporary clothing. Casting and where a performance is held may also affect delivery of lines. For this reason, minor changes in the wording are permissible, to put the actors at ease and help them better relate to a particular audience.

Although these dramatic readings can be produced as a series, each individual sketch stands on its own and may be used as the catalyst for a sermon, discussion, or integrated into a musical program or Easter cantata. The Gamaliel sketch, for instance, provides an excellent bridge between Easter Resurrection and the Day of Pentecost. The manner in which each dramatic reading is presented is part of the creative process. In each instance, the aim is to provoke thought and bring people to a personal faith in Jesus Christ as Savior and Lord.

AT THE FOOT OF THE CROSS

Easter Dramatic Readings

by Barbara Dan

12 Character Sketches

Listed in random order for use during the Lenten Season and during Easter Week Sermons, Devotions, Special Easter Programs, and Communion

The Rich Young Ruler

Which of us does not regret some decision we've made? Or not made? Some opportunity we've passed over. Hindsight is 20/20, they say. Just about all of us—I see some of you nodding your heads—have wondered, What would my life have been like if I had, say, married Mary instead of Rachel?

What if I had finished my university training before getting married?

What if I had chosen a different profession?

In my case, I had often wondered: What if I had not walked away from Jesus that day when He told me, "Sell all you have, give to the poor, and follow me."

My response to that question still haunts me to this day.

I know some people probably believe it was because I couldn't give up my wealth. But deep down inside, because everything had always been handed to me all my life, I had often wondered if poverty was really the issue, and whether I could have made it on my own.

I now recognize my underlying emotion was fear. Fear and a lack of self-worth were the underlying reasons for my rejection of Jesus' invitation to follow Him. Sure, on the surface, I sounded confident. I had always been obedient and respectful toward my parents. Like all teens, I struggled with secret thoughts of rebellion. I guess that's what prompted me to approach Jesus in the beginning.

Yet something was missing from my life. I had observed all the Commandments. I was a model son. But always in the back of my head,

I wondered if I could be my own person and enjoy an identity among my friends that was totally mine. My parents' friends referred to me as "Aaron and Leah's son." I wanted to be *me*!

But who was I? Who was I really?

I wanted desperately to discover what I was capable of becoming.

Maybe I was raised to be cautious by overly protective parents, but the idea of giving up all the benefits of wealth, prestige, and family reputation, and stepping out for Jesus without a backup system scared me.

What if I failed? What if my religious fervor turned out to be a pipedream? I had to be certain I didn't align myself politically and religiously with a lost cause!

After all, Jesus was a highly controversial figure. Some people claimed He was the promised Messiah, who would deliver us from our enemies and usher in a thousand years reign of peace and prosperity. Nothing from His own mouth suggested that was His primary agenda. With so many people stirred up, it only made good sense not to jump too fast and become one of His followers without giving the idea long and serious thought.

After all, Jesus expected me to "sell all my possessions" and give to the poor. That in itself is a radical idea. Anyone knows the poor got that way by not working. Who has not seen drunks staggering about with the blind shakes at noon? Our marketplace is full of unfortunate human specimens, beggars and thieves among their number.

No, handing over my wealth to such worthless scum was unthinkable! An irresponsible thing to do.

Not that I haven't done my share of charitable giving. But to give money to poor people without requiring an accounting? ***[shakes head]*** That would be downright foolhardy!

So I walked away from Jesus' invitation to become one of His disciples.

Don't look so shocked! In my place, you'd have done the same thing. Come on . . . Admit it!

I grew up believing wealth was a sign of God's favor. I was born into a life of privilege for a reason. And I lived a good clean life, obeying the

Commandments, respecting my elders, and thus had secured a place of respect and honor among the power brokers of my day.

Although young, I knew everyone worth knowing. I had formed political and business connections. I was engaged to marry the daughter of a powerful merchant, with trade routes all over the known world. People said I had it made! I was set for life. And probably they were right.

But all the insulation from problems and cares of this world still left something lacking, only I just couldn't lay my finger on what was missing.

Something deep inside kept nagging at me, like a dog gnawing a bone and never finding the meat. My soul seemed famished. Often I would pause in my busy schedule to reflect on Jesus.

Passover week: He was in the city along with thousands of spiritual pilgrims. People came from far and wide to Jerusalem. It was time once more to celebrate God's deliverance of His people from their oppressors and from slavery.

This Passover, people thronged the city with a new sense of excitement. "Hosanna!" they shouted. "Blessed is He who comes in the Name of the Lord!"

The hope for Messianic intervention was never higher.

Many felt the time was right. The Romans ruled with an iron hand.

Who didn't want freedom? ***I*** certainly did. I was tired of the government breathing down my back. We were being taxed to death!

When I learned of Jesus' arrival, I was jubilant. Perhaps He ***was*** the Messiah. Our promised Savior. Family contacts in the religious community all roundly criticized Jesus, but among friends my own age, I also heard more hopeful whispers that the Roman rule might somehow be overthrown.

I decided that as soon as I had eaten the Passover feast with my parents, I would seek out Jesus and renew our acquaintance.

Friday morning: I awoke to learn I was too late.

Jesus had been arrested and in two speedy trials, both held in the dead of night, the Chief Priests and Pharisees ***and*** our Roman enemies had condemned Jesus to die. He was to be executed that very day as a common criminal!

Needless to say, I was shocked. "How can this be?" I demanded of my father. "Such a verdict is unjust. The Man is innocent of any wrongdoing!"

My father, annoyed at having his breakfast interrupted, set down his spoon with a disapproving scowl. "This scallywag Jesus, whom you so hotly defend, claims to be the eternal God. 'Before Abraham was, I AM,' he told his accusers. He is either a madman, or a scoundrel and a charlatan. Either way, His death is no great loss."

Horrified by my father's harsh attitude, I fled the house.

Jesus, who had offered me His friendship and wisdom, was about to die. Time was running out. I had figured I had all the time in the world to make up my mind about whether to follow Jesus or not.

Now, stumbling through the streets, bumping up against hot and sweaty bodies, I realized that I, like my father, was guilty of a complacent and self-serving spirit. I was guilty of unbridled pride. Of wanting to control my wealth, dictate its use, or squander it, according to my own will.

Instinctively Jesus had known my Achilles heel. He saw me for what I was—my strengths, my weaknesses. And I had rejected Him with great sorrow in my heart. But not enough to repent. No, not enough sorrow and remorse to repent of my selfishness and self-preoccupation.

What a fool I was! I claimed to err on the side of caution, when all the time I was the victim of self-deception. I prided myself on making reasonable, rational decisions, when in actuality, I was a phony. Claiming I kept the Commandments and presenting myself as righteous, while refusing to carry out the spirit of the Mosaic law!

I did not love my neighbor—unless being nice to my social peers could increase my net worth. The reason I didn't give to the poor was simple: I ***was*** better off and therefore regarded myself as more pleasing in God's sight than ordinary citizens. What a bumptious, conceited hypocrite I had become!

That brief revelation showed me just how strong a grip sin had on my life, and threw me into turmoil such as I had never experienced before. I suddenly saw the destructive path I had been traveling.

And I knew I needed deliverance from what was ***inside*** me, more than I needed a political Messiah! I wanted to be made a new man, free of my destructive nature.

"Oh, Jesus, forgive me," I cried, but my words were lost in the noise of the crowd that bore me along. Suddenly I realized I had made my way up the hill to the Place of the Skull, Golgotha, where the vilest criminals were put to death by the Romans.

And there, arms outstretched on a cross, was Jesus. Jesus who had sought to befriend me, not because I had money, but because I needed a true Friend and a purpose in life.

Jesus—beaten and bloody, fighting for breath, yet very much in command of Himself. His eyes rested on me for a second, and my heart broke. I buried my face in my hands, crying like a baby at the injustice of His death.

I had become so much a part of the way the world operates, and here was the proof: It was a crooked, exploitive system that manipulated the lives of men and women like pawns in a game of chess. A game played by the privileged classes, but a cruel one for the downtrodden. I, by my complacency, was partly to blame for His death.

Jesus hung between two criminals, and I wondered what circumstances had led them to such a terrible end. Without doubt, they were guilty, had committed heinous crimes. But what if their lives had been different? Could an education or a trade have made honest men of them? Too late now, but still I wondered if men like these, and their families, were among the poor Jesus had wanted me to give my worldly possessions to. My burden of guilt grew heavier, as I realized my sin. I had neglected the needs of my fellow man.

As I stood before Jesus, blood running down His face from the crown of thorns He wore, my heart cried out for some Authority, perhaps God

Himself, to halt the proceedings and rescue Jesus from His pain and torment. But none came. No one spoke up. At the foot of His cross, soldiers were casting dice, gambling for his clothing. The crowd was divided. Some threw garbage and foul curses. Others stood quietly praying.

The two thieves cursed vilely with every tortured breath. And then Jesus uttered a prayer that will haunt me to my dying day: "Father, forgive them, for they don't know what they're doing."

Who was He praying for? The thieves? The men who had inflicted such excruciating pain? The chief priests with their mocking smiles? The streetwalkers and pickpockets working the crowd? Pilate, safe behind heavily guarded palace walls, who had given in to political pressure? Or was He asking forgiveness for me? For the nation of Israel? Could His forgiveness extend to the Romans? To people in other lands as well?

Who was this Man Jesus? And then I remembered my father saying that Jesus claimed, "Before Abraham was, I AM."

As thunder and lightning rumbled over the city, the Truth came to me in a flash: Only God's own Son, dying for sins He didn't commit, was capable of such forgiveness and love in the presence of His enemies.

Passover! Jesus was our Paschal Lamb! This was no martyr's death. It was the direct result of a world of evil pitted against a righteous and holy God. Jesus was the innocent Lamb of God. His shed blood alone could save us from the bondage of sin. What amazing love! Who but God would bother to save a wretch like me! Alleluia!

I still cannot explain what made me fall face down in the dirt, overcome by a sense of my spiritual poverty, or why I broke into incoherent weeping and utterances of praise, all in the same breath. His suffering was for me! For you! It was not for nothing that He died. Waves of His love washed over me, as Jesus spoke a tender farewell to his mother and one of his disciples.

He spoke through cracked swollen lips: "Dear woman, here is your son," and directing his gaze to his disciple John, said, "Here is your mother."

I was amazed. Jesus, stripped naked by the injustices of life, sharing a gift more precious than gold with His mother and a friend: His Love.

A king might give away jewels and a kingdom at his death. Jesus gave better gifts. Riches that fed the soul. Forgiveness. Understanding and comfort to an unworthy thief: "Today you will be with me in Paradise." And now . . . love.

Soon after that, Jesus cried out, "***Eloi, Eloi, Lama sabach-thani***. My God, my God, ***why*** have you forsaken me?"

Struggling with grief and shock, I got to my feet. Even God had forsaken Jesus. The sky was dark overhead. In His darkest hour Jesus was alone. The agony of His suffering filled me with such shame that I had to turn away my face. I couldn't bear to look. Finally, Jesus cried out in a loud voice, "It is finished!"

And in some way I still didn't understand, Jesus died to liberate those who were all their lives held captive to sin.

My friend, Jesus died for me. And He died for you.

Son of a Thief

(played by a teenager, perhaps surrounded by two or three of his siblings, all younger, all dressed in burlap rags and shoeless)

I am a nobody. Just a face in the crowd. Brought up in poverty. An orphan, along with my brother and sister here.

Mother and the two babies died of cholera a few years ago.

My Dad, he tried his best to keep what was left of our family together. But for a laboring man with no special skills, finding work to feed a hungry family wasn't easy. Soon we fell on hard times. Dad took to the streets, stealing food and robbing houses by night. But like all thieves, he eventually got caught.

And now he has paid with his life.

I saw him die. Him and his accomplice.

And that other Man, the one they call Jesus.

Me and my brother and sister went to tell Dad goodbye.

He wasn't such a bad Dad. He wasn't perfect. He did bad stuff and got drunk sometimes and got into fights. But he was all we had. He was my Dad, and he did the best he could by us.

So we walked up Mount Calvary, hoping to say goodbye and wondering what was going to become of us kids.

I'm not very old, but I knew it was up to me now to take care of my brother and sister. And I knew that if I had to lie and steal to do it, I would. I just hope I wouldn't kill anybody, because dying was a mean, ugly business, the way the Romans do it.

I didn't ever want to get caught.

Don't get me wrong. I didn't want to be a criminal. My Dad didn't either. He didn't just wake up one morning and say to himself, "I want to steal me some fish." Times were hard, and him and us kids, we were always hungry. Sometimes our bellies were so empty, our insides rubbed together like gravel and sand.

(Changes subject)

Do you know what it's like to be crucified? It's the most terrible way to die. It's not quick, like getting your head chopped off, or somebody sticking a knife in your heart, or having a scaffold fall and a rope choke you to death—Nothing quick like that, where you're dead before you have a chance to think about all your sins and what a mess you've made of your life.

Uh-uh. Dying the Roman way is pure torture.

I watched them soldiers beat the living daylights out of my Dad first. Then they crucified him. He cussed them bad. But it only made them laugh.

They hammered big spikes through his hands and feet, and with every blow, the screams got louder and louder!

I could hardly keep from screaming myself. It hurt so much to watch what they were doing to my Dad.

And then they raised him up on this cross-piece with his arms stretched tight. When they slammed the cross-piece into place on top of the post, all the breath was knocked out of him. He started fighting for breath, and I'm tellin' you, all the bitterness in my Dad's life just spewed out like dirty water out of a sewer. He cussed God, and he cussed the crowd.

He even cussed me! He said he was sorry I was ever born. That he hated me and my brother and sister. It was *our* fault, he said, because if it weren't for having so many mouths to feed, he would never have—

(Hangs head.) I tell you, I was so ashamed. I know I'm nothing special, but for my own Dad to say that in front of that crowd of riff-raff—! It really hurt.

I just wanted to get out of there—fast!

I wanted to cover my ears and hide from the stream of curses.

I wanted to grab my sister and brother's hands and run away. Far away.

But I couldn't.

He was still my Dad, no matter what.

Besides, he was where I would probably end up myself, if I wasn't careful. It was a lesson I wanted to burn into my brain and never forget.

So I stood with everyone else. People watching an execution say the strangest things, you know? Like one lady kept saying, "Thank you, Jesus. Thank you, Jesus."

Thank Him for what? It seemed a stupid thing to say to a dying Man.

One of the soldiers said, "This man committed no crime."

But then a priest from the temple said, "He claims He's the Son of the Most High God. Blasphemy! For this He deserves to die!"

So I began watching the Man named Jesus.

He didn't act like my Dad or the other thief.

Jesus was in just as much pain. No, I take that back. He suffered more. The soldiers had scourged him with a whip, and blood was running down his face from the crown of long thorns they had shoved down on his forehead.

Every so often, someone would reach out and touch the post close to where His feet were nailed. They would talk to this Jesus, and somehow He found the strength to offer a word of comfort. Other times, He lifted up His head and prayed.

He said, "Father, forgive them, for they don't know what they're doing."

Wow! That really made me listen!

I was a sinner in need of forgiveness.

So was my Dad—big time.

But did my Dad ask Jesus for forgiveness?

No, I am ashamed to say he didn't.

But as time went on, and the end of their suffering drew near, the *other* thief called to Jesus, "Remember me when you come into your kingdom."

And Jesus told him, "I tell you the truth, today you will be with me in Paradise."

Can you imagine? "Today!" In spite of the crimes he had committed.

How I wished that for my Dad, too.

Earlier, Jesus had turned to his mother in the crowd and said, "Dear Mother, behold your son," indicating the young man standing next to her. And then He told his friend, "Behold your mother."

In that moment, I wished he would tell me where to turn for a mother. I needed someone older to love me. My Dad was dying, and with his dying breath, he had disowned me.

Who could I look to for help?

The day grew darker. Storm clouds on the horizon settled over my spirit like fear of the unknown. And then at about the ninth hour of the day, Jesus cried out in a loud voice, "My God, my God, why have; you forsaken me?"

That's how I felt, too. My Dad had turned away from me. And here was this Jesus, Who forgave his enemies—all the mockers and scoffers and sinners. Even thieves!

Jesus, who saw to the needs of His mother and His friend, who was not much older than me. Jesus, who promised a place in Paradise to a thief.

He was a Man of sorrows, who felt the pain of others, even when He Himself was dying!

In that moment, as He cried out to His Father in Heaven, I found myself loving Him.

He was the kind of Friend I needed. Someone who knew what it was to be forsaken and abandoned, to feel so cut off from God and human friendship. I wanted to know Him better, but time had run out.

In spite of feeling that God had turned His back on Him, Jesus still committed His spirit to His Father in Heaven, and then, in a last torturous gasp, He cried out, “It is finished!”

I was alone in the world, faced with raising my brother and sister.

(To audience:)

I am poor. A nobody in the eyes of the world—

A nameless face in the crowd to most people.

But I feel different about myself now, because today I met a Man named Jesus.

He understands. He gives me hope.

With His help, I can get through today. And tomorrow? . . Paradise!

That’s what He promised!

Andrew and Peter

(A Dialogue)

PETER:

Where have you been, Andrew?! I've been worried sick!

ANDREW:

(portray as slow and deliberate in speech)

I was "out there" with Jesus.

PETER *(alarmed)***:**

What? You went out to the Place of the Skull? Are you crazy? What if they had arrested you, too?

ANDREW:

Don't be mad at me, Peter. After all the bad things you told me about what they did to Jesus, I figured He needed a friend closeby.

PETER *(guilt and remorse surfacing)*:

Andrew, forgive me. I didn't mean to bite your head off. It's just that . . . Well, I'm so ashamed. I denied Him—three times! Denied I ever knew him!

ANDREW *(pats his brother's shoulder)*:

That's OK, Peter. You were afraid.

PETER *(amazed)*:

And you weren't?

ANDREW *(shrugs sheepishly)*:

Yeah, I was, kind of. Those soldiers were scary with their whips. They treated Jesus mean, and those other guys they cru—crucified.

PETER:

Then why did you go?

ANDREW *(smiles)*:

That's easy. Nobody ever notices ***me***. I don't talk good as you, and—and I'm shorter than you, so I don't stick out. *(laughs)* Who would notice a dumb cluck like me in the crowd?

PETER:

Well, you're certainly braver than me. So, tell me what happened, Andrew.

ANDREW:

The crowds pushed me a lot. It was hard getting through to where Jesus was. People were yelling and cursing. They said bad things about Jesus! Mean things, like, "Why don't He save Himself?" and—oh, I don't know. Well, that made me mad, Peter. *(tears in his voice)* They hated Him for . . . . for no reason! While . . . while the soldiers were hammering nails through His feet and hands and tying Him to that cross, people threw garbage and spit on Him.

PETER:

Oh! God, forgive me! If anyone deserved to have garbage thrown at him, it's me! I should have been there to fight for him. Instead, I hid.

ANDREW *(placating):*

It's OK, Peter. Jesus is still your friend.

PETER:

He's dead! It cost Him His life, because I wasn't quicker with my sword. If only James and John and I had kept watch in the Garden, as He asked! We could have warned Him in time and helped Him escape.

ANDREW *(shakes head)*:

I don't know about that, Peter. Jesus told us He was going to die, remember?

PETER *(looking grim)*:

I know, but I still think I could have prevented His arrest and what followed.

ANDREW:

The soldiers nearly skinned Jesus alive with their whips. It hurt me just to look at Him. He was bleeding and dirty. I almost didn't recognize Him, he was so beat up. Worse than any fishermen's brawl I've ever been in.

PETER *(rubs knuckles)*:

Yeah. Before we met Jesus, we got in some pretty bad fights.

ANDREW:

You have such big fists; they used to say, "Watch out! Here comes the Big Fisherman," remember?

PETER:

I gave up fighting when Jesus came down to where we were mending our nets. "Follow me, men, and I'll make you fishers of men!" What a great Friend He was. *(Turns morose again.)* And I turned out to be such a rotten liar!

ANDREW *(gently)*:

We're none of us perfect.

PETER:

I can't excuse my behavior. What I did was the act of a craven coward! I betrayed my best friend!

ANDREW:

He was my Best Friend, too.

PETER:

You've been a better friend to Him than me. Always. Remember when He called you "a man without guile"? You have a heart of gold, Andrew.

ANDREW *(nods)*:

I'm not complicated like you, Peter, that's all.

PETER:

Thank God you're not like me. It's not in your nature to lie or say hateful things. Jesus said that about you the first time He met you. He read you exactly right. Me, too. He warned me that I would betray Him. "Before the cock crows twice, you will deny me three times," He said. I tell you, Andrew, I may look like a big man on the outside, but inside, I feel like a scared little kid.

ANDREW:

You do?

PETER:

I'm no good. When the chips were down, and my best Friend needed my help, all I cared about was saving my own skin. I denied I ever knew Him.

ANDREW:

I still like you, Peter.

PETER:

Thanks.

ANDREW:

I think Jesus still cares for you, too.

PETER:

What makes you think that?

ANDREW:

When people were treating Him so mean, and spitting on Him, and throwing rocks and trash at Him on the cross, He prayed, "Father, forgive them, for they know not what they do." And when one of the thieves beside Him asked Jesus to remember him in Paradise—just ***remember***, not rescue or save—Jesus gave him an IOU promise.

PETER:

What are you talking about?! Jesus had nothing left to give anyone! He was penniless. The best He could expect was a pauper's grave.

ANDREW *(really excited)*:

No, Peter! A rich man—Joseph, one of the Sanhedrin Council—buried Jesus. Yes, he did! In his very own grave.

PETER:

You sure about that?

ANDREW *(nods)*:

I know it for a fact. But before Jesus died, He promised the thief that he would be with Him that very day in Paradise! Not a place of torment, which he pro'bly deserved for all his crimes, but Paradise! Imagine that!

PETER *(skeptical)*:

Are you sure?

ANDREW:

Yes, He did! And if Jesus loved that thief enough to . . . to promise him a place in Paradise, I'm sure He has a place for you and me in Paradise, too!

PETER *(reflects on the Last Supper)*:

At supper last night, Jesus said, "I go to prepare a place for you, that where I am, you may be also . . ." Andrew, thank you! You've given me new hope!

ANDREW:

John was there at the foot of the cross, too, with Jesus' mother. Would you like me to show you where they buried His body?

PETER *(peers out front)*:

Night has fallen. It's pitch dark, and the Sabbath is upon us.

ANDREW:

John and I will show you in the morning.

PETER:

When the Sabbath is over, we shall go see our Master.

[They EXIT together, arms around each other's shoulders.]

Princess Salome

[ENTERS dancing in a swirl of sheer veils (sheer drapes work well over a simple dress). Bracelets jangling, she prances up to the microphone, animated and full of herself. She divests herself of her face veil, making a joke of her persona. She's fast talking and nervous.]

Hello, everybody! Remember me? Salome. You know! The favorite party girl at all my uncle's lavish parties. Oh, good, you *do* remember! My mother Herodias and her husband, Herod Antipas, used to throw parties that were absolutely to die for. *Any*one who was anybody made a point of being there.

Of course, I was the main attraction. Men came from miles around to see me dance. They worshipped at my feet—*(pulls up edge of her skirt and wiggles her toes at audience)*—How do you like my arches? Pretty cute, huh? Men lavished me with gifts just for the pleasure of my company during dinner.

Lots of traveling diplomats and Roman potentates came through the palace in Galilee. True, we were a little off the beaten path, but a good party draws people from far and wide. A never ending parade of military officers supplied the ladies from Herod's court with dancing partners. We even entertained Governor Pilate on occasion!

(Sighs) Yes, Mother used to put on a really big spread—all the best foods. Seafood and salty eel, dried fruits and melons . . . mountains of fresh grapes, brought in by caravan. I tell you, our guests were well taken care of.

And, my my my! How the wine flowed! Mother's parties used to go on for days!

Capernaum itself was a little boring, but I managed to amuse myself. *(Looks coyly at the men in the audience.)* Both my husbands were ideally suited for a venturesome princess like myself. Herod expected me to welcome important guests, and so I did have something of a reputation among the palace women.

(Tosses her head.) What do I care what people say behind my back? I was just doing my job. If I didn't keep my stepfather happy, my husband I would have been exiled so fast it would have made our heads spin!

So you see, celebrity has its place, even if people say bad things about you.

Anyway, it's good you remember me. I would be disappointed if you'd forgotten me so soon. After all, I've become the personification of eroticism and self-indulgence. *(pout in voice)* It's all because I tried to defend my mother Herodias's reputation.

Could she help it, if my father Philip, her first husband, was brother to her second husband, Herod Antipas? It was a logical next step to marry Herod Antipas. After all, he was the tetrarch ruler. So Dad stepped out of the picture, and she married Herod.

Anyway, how was she to know it was against Mosaic Law? She was just trying to better her circumstances. And believe me, a woman has to look out for herself in a male dominated culture. ***I*** know!

Well, it was bad enough having the religious leaders in an uproar, but then along came John the Baptist, that uncouth preacher from the hill country, turning the common people against us. Can you imagine his nerve—criticizing my mother, a prominent social lioness? She was known far and wide for her impeccable manners and taste.

So along comes this scraggly, unwashed itinerant preacher and his rag-tag followers, standing in the town square and demanding that Herod and my mother "repent and be baptized" in the muddy waters of the Jordan! The nerve of this man to humiliate my mother.

Mother was furious, and well, I admit I had too much wine that night. But when she asked me to dance, I pulled out all the stops and gave the performance of my life. You should have seen Herod Antipas' eyes! He got really excited by my dance of the seven veils. If he hadn't been married to my mother, I have no doubt he would have proposed to me on the spot.

But he didn't. He saw the effect my dancing had on his male guests, and being a smart politician, he decided to show off his wealth and generosity toward me for entertaining his guests so well.

As his stepdaughter, I knew I could wheedle a really nice gift out of him anytime. So I played him like a fish on a line, until he promised me up to "half his kingdom." I tell you, he was putty in my hands. Anything I asked for in front of his guests was mine. I was about to ask for his villa on the coast, but then I saw Mother's eyes. She was smiling, but inside, I could sense her pain and sadness. And I knew why.

(Shrugs) So I asked for the head of John the Baptist on a platter.

At first, Herod refused. But I knew he had to keep his promise, "up to half his kingdom," or his guests would think poorly of him. Again I insisted.

Now, John was already under arrest, lodged below the banquet hall in the dungeon, because of his incessant preaching. But Herod, for some reason, was afraid of John. But finally, Herod agreed to my request.

The order was sent below, and a short time later—I recall I was dining with the vice-consul from Ethiopia—the music came to an abrupt halt.

Voices hushed with a gasp, as the chief executioner came bowing and placed before me a large platter with the head of John the Baptist on it.

The eyes, half-open, stared at me accusingly. The long hair still dripping in blood, the sharp features of the prophet were blanched with the pallor of death.

I had avenged my mother. I had killed to show where my loyalties lay.

I felt like throwing up, the image before me was so gruesome.

Yet I had insisted on this as my reward for dancing. I knew I couldn't let my true feelings show. Even though I had no stomach for such a grisly murder, I could not show my horror or regret. Every eye was upon me. I had forced Herod Antipas to commit this despicable deed, and now I was expected to show my gratitude for his generosity.

Actually, the sacrifice of John's life was not a gift. It had cost Herod nothing! But it ***had*** cost John the Baptist his life, and that was troubling—even to a jaded party girl like me.

I had participated in many mind and soul-numbing acts, including orgies and extra-marital affaires. I had lied and engaged in political intrigue, carrying treasonous messages between the Romans and the Israeli leaders. But I had never poisoned anyone. True, I had arranged to miscarry two pregnancies that were *unpardonably* inconvenient, but I had never before stared into the face of an enemy I had killed.

The guests were watching. Waiting to see how I would react.

I laughed to show my pleasure. I snatched John's head up in my hands, hair sticky with blood. I kissed him on those ghoulish, slack lips.

There! That should prove how steady my nerves were. That should satisfy all Mother's fine guests! "A good time was had by all!" I could imagine them saying later. "Herodias and her daughter sure know how to throw a party."

Inside I was shaking like a palm leaf in a hurricane. My hands were sweaty, as I set the head back on the tray. "Bring on the jugglers! Send in the clowns," I called, and the musicians struck up a lively tune.

Late that night, when the palace guests were too drunk with wine to notice my departure, I had my personal servants carry me down to the lake, where I bathed. Only, I couldn't get ***clean!*** Even perfumed soaps and rubbing myself all over with coarse sand, till my skin was raw, couldn't get rid of my guilt and shame. I was not just a woman who had compromised herself to stay in the limelight, I was a murderer.

And there was no god I could call on, among all the hundreds of images that lined the streets. What I had done was unforgivable. I had sunk so low, even ***I*** couldn't stand my own company.

In the months that followed, I tried to pretend nothing had changed, that the death of John the Baptist meant nothing to me.

"He deserved to die," I told people who asked how I felt about his death. I drank more, took new lovers. Nothing eased the fear and guilt. I sought oblivion in the opium pipe, but my dreams only grew more troubling. I was lost, though careful not to reveal my true feelings.

Like most residents of Galilee, I knew John the Baptist had a distant cousin who also went about the region preaching. A man called Jesus. Low-born, a carpenter's son, according to palace gossip. Sometimes I overheard my maids talk among themselves of His miracles and strange teachings about forgiveness and loving one's enemies.

Unbelievable rubbish! Nobody loves their enemies. They kill them.

Just as I had John the Baptist killed for criticizing my mother.

Jesus' teachings brought no comfort to my heart, believe me!

Nobody could forgive what I had done. I had no clear idea what would happen when I died, but I knew the After-Life would be a place of even greater torment. *(Waves her hand dismissively)* But never mind death!

Living only got harder with every passing day. I was constantly afraid. John's head, dripping blood on my gown, haunted my nightmares. I stayed up nights, pacing, afraid to lie down, for fear I might die in my sleep, or be killed. I didn't trust my servants. What if one of them was a secret follower of this man Jesus?

I knew, if I ever met this Jesus, He would spit on me and strangle me for what I had done to his cousin John. Every time I left the palace, I was terrified. What if I ran into Him or a crowd of His "disciples"? Thoughts of ambush and revenge made my heart race in wild panic as I passed through the streets.

Nearly three years passed. I aged a lot. I drank to excess. Sure, I still danced, but only to appease my mother's friends. I no longer had a dancer's heart of joy. But I had my role to play in the political circles in which I moved.

Every spring, everyone heads to Jerusalem for the Passover. I was an invited guest at the palace of Herod Agrippa, related to me through my stepfather, Herod Antipas. Imagine my surprise when I awakened one morning to learn that my nemesis, Jesus of Nazareth, had been arrested the night before. He had been tried and found guilty, condemned to death on a charge of blasphemy by the Jewish religious leaders. They got themselves all worked up, because Jesus said He and the Father were one, and claimed He was deity.

Instantly I was all ears. Agrippa said Jesus was stirring up civil unrest in the city, and with the crowds pouring into Jerusalem for the Passover, Governor Pilate had to act quickly to appease the Jewish leaders and keep the peace.

Rumor had it that Jesus was the Messiah, the Promised One who would deliver the Jews from political oppression. The general opinion was that if it took the death of one man to quell a riot, then so be it.

The Carpenter from Nazareth was being crucified that very morning by Roman soldiers.

The man I feared was about to die! You can imagine my excitement. At last I would be free of my fear of sudden death or ambush.

Jesus would no longer be able to hunt me down or spoil my dreams.

Excusing myself from the other palace guests, I summoned my litter and climbed inside. Drawing the curtains closed, I rubbed my hands with glee. Jesus would have no more power over me! I would be able to sleep again!

After all, dead men have no power over the living!

My bearers carried me quickly through the crowded streets. All my bodyguard had to do was announce, "Make way for the Princess Salome!" and people scurried out of the way.

Up the hill we went. I was somewhat shaken by the litter's rapid progress up Golgotha, where criminals were put to death. My heart was hammering with excitement. As I drew nearer, I heard shouts of "Crucify Him!" and "Let Him save Himself, if He is truly the Son of God!"

Suddenly my bearers stopped. We had arrived.

Of course, no woman of nobility steps down onto the bare dirt. And so my bodyguard spread a small Persian carpet so that I could descend in proper style. I was swathed in veils, protected from the impolite and condemning stares of the men standing around. The only other women present were common hags, probably relatives or pick-pockets. The smell of unwashed bodies was overwhelming, and I fought a wave of nausea.

Being out of my element, I felt a bit uneasy. But I had come with servants and my bodyguard, so personal safety was not a real issue. Several Roman soldiers were there to keep the peace, as well.

So why had I come?

I wanted to add my words of scorn to the mocking taunts of this rabble crowd. I wanted to spit upon this Jesus. "Do unto others before they can do it to you," was a philosophy most dear to my heart.

"Which one is Jesus?" I asked the Centurion who approached. I realized that I stood out among the crudely garbed men like a bright parrot against an adobe mud wall.

"That one." He jabbed his thumb toward a wooden cross. Above the crucified man's head, the nature of his crime was inscribed: "Jesus of Nazareth, King of the Jews." The other two men were being crucified for the crime of "theft."

Quickly dismissing the two thieves from mind, I stepped forward, letting my servants scramble to keep my feet out of the dirt the best they could. I had to see this Jesus! Look Him straight in the eye. I stood where He could not help but see me.

The minute He recognized me, I was sure He would begin to condemn me and curse me. Part of me wanted Him to sneer and curse me, for that would justify my mocking Him in return.

'Go ahead, Jesus,' I thought. 'Call me a wicked Jezebel, an unfaithful wife, a liar, a heartless woman! Tell the world what You think of me.'

Blood ran down from His brow. The crown of thorns cut into His forehead, and sweat and dirt marred His bruised face. Deep purple bruises covered His face and body. He was well muscled—evidence that He had been a healthy male before the Romans subjected him to flogging. A pattern of stripes criss-crossed his body, and the flesh was torn and jagged, in places ripped from His body by the metal tips on the end of each lash.

I had looked into the dead eyes of His cousin John, and yet, when I looked up at Jesus, arms stretched taut against the splintered timbers of His cross, I saw a Man whose eyes were totally alive! The men on either side of him were groaning and pleading for mercy.

But Jesus, though in excruciating pain, showed a calm resignation.

I signaled my servants to move closer. I wanted to touch the feet nailed to that cross.

Seeing my intent, the Centurion laid a restraining hand on my arm. Decent women did not attend executions. How could the Centurion know that beneath my rich royal garments beat a heart more unclean than the worst outcasts in Israel—the lepers?

My look of scorn showed the Centurion his place, and he stepped back. Yes, there *are* advantages to being high-born! I, Princess Salome, go where I please, and do as I wish.

But before I could actually reach up and lay my hand on the feet of Jesus, He spoke: "Father, forgive them, for they know not what they do."

The gentle compassion in His voice took my breath away.

He knew my great sin! Yet he spoke of forgiveness.

Jesus had been beaten . . . subjected to torture. He was being put to death by the cruelest form of execution. How was it possible that He could still speak of forgiveness?

I went weak in the knees. Right there, in the filth of spilled blood and urine and spittle, surrounded by a crowd reeking of sweat, I fell to my knees sobbing. I could not fathom such love! I was a vile sinner, weighed down by crimes against humanity. My heart was as wicked as every other sinner who'd come to make fun of Jesus. He had not been born to a life of privilege, as I had been. Yet His gracious words were spoken like those of a King!

He saw my sin and forgave! Oh, what mercy! What amazing love!

Jesus did not deserve to die. He was no murderer. ***I*** was! *I* was the guilty one! And He forgave . . .

What transpired next I cannot say for certain. One minute I was on my knees, begging forgiveness. Then my servants were lifting me to my feet and carrying me through the crowd, back to my litter. I was so overcome with grief that I offered no resistance. But I wanted to *stay!*

I wanted to kneel at the feet of Jesus forever.

Herod Agrippa might be the puppet king of the Jews, doing the will of Roman captors, but I knew—I ***knew*** that I had just met the Eternal One, the true King of the Jews. The Mighty One. My Deliverer!

Lazarus, Martha and Mary

[MAY BE USED IN A COMMUNION SERVICE]

[All three ENTER, bowed under the weight of grief as they discuss the death of their friend, Jesus.]

LAZARUS:

He's dead. If I hadn't seen Him die with my own eyes, I wouldn't believe it was possible!

MARY:

I know, Lazarus. My heart is broken, too. I never expected Jesus to die. Especially not as a convicted felon.

MARTHA:

It doesn't make sense to me either. Jesus raised Lazarus from the grave, so we know He has power over death. Why did He have to die?

MARY:

Oh, Martha, He didn't *have* to die. He *chose* to die. But *why*? *(Turns to her brother.)* Do you have any idea why this might be, Lazarus?

LAZARUS:

Mary, I have no idea. But He must have had some larger purpose in mind why He allowed the politicians to put Him to death. *(Then, in anger)* On trumped up charges, don't forget *that!*

MARTHA:

Hush, Lazarus. Subversive talk about our leaders will only get us in more trouble. And now that Jesus is gone, what's the point?

MARY:

All you two ever wanted was to bring the Messiah to power and to overthrow foreign rule!

LAZARUS:

Jesus was the Messiah! If He hadn't died, I know He would have delivered us from our enemies.

MARTHA:

Well, it's futile to think He can help Israel now.

MARY:

You both talk as if death is so final!

LAZARUS:

Not so. Remember, Jesus raised me from the dead, removing my fear of death forever. But I know I will face physical death again. This body still gets creaky to remind me how temporary this life is. But as long as I live in this flesh, I want a better life for myself and my countrymen. You can't blame me for wanting freedom, now can you?

MARY:

No, of course not.

MARTHA:

What I can't figure out is why Jesus, who had the power of life and death, allowed the Romans and the chief priests to arrest Him and kill Him like a common criminal.

MARY:

Some things we may never figure out, Mary. I guess that's where faith comes into play.

MARTHA:

Faith—bah! How you talk, Mary. Our dear friend Jesus is dead, crucified on a cross. The torture He suffered was barbaric and cruel! I'm sorry if I sound bitter, but His death was such a miscarriage of justice. Frankly, I've had it up to here with the powers that be. *(Makes a slashing gesture across her neck)*

MARY:

But surely we haven't seen the last of Jesus yet. Remember His shout of triumph when He yielded up His spirit to His heavenly Father? He wasn't conquered by evil, and neither should we.

LAZARUS: *(visibly grieving)*

I wish I could go out to that graveyard right now, and do for Him what He did for me. I would shout, "Jesus, come forth from the grave!"

MARTHA:

(bitterness showing in her critical attitude)

Well, you might as well forget it! Making a spectacle of yourself won't bring Him back. Jesus had the power of His Father to raise the dead. You don't. We are just ordinary human beings.

MARY:

I never felt “ordinary” when I was around Jesus . . .

LAZARUS:

Truer words were never spoken! What joy and hope I felt whenever Jesus came to visit. He made my troubles light, like they’d roll off my back. Oh, how I loved Him. He was a Friend I can never replace. Like no other.

MARY:

I know what: Let’s invite other friends of His into our home—right now! Martha and I will serve refreshments, while we all share what Jesus has done for us, and how He has changed our lives. What a wonderful way to honor Him for the friendship and love He has shown to each of us!

At this point, ideally on a Sunday when communion is served, the congregation can be invited to testify briefly about their love of the Lord Jesus Christ, as they partake of the fruit of the vine and the bread together.

Caiaphas the High Priest

SCRIBE:

(following Caiaphas around with notepad, jotting notes)

So tell me, Caiaphas, what's the real scoop about this Jesus?

CAIAPHAS:

(flattered by the attention, but playing down his involvement)

Jesus?

SCRIBE:

Yeah, you know. Jesus of Nazareth. The guy you and the Sanhedrin interrogated behind closed doors last night.

CAIAPHAS *(clears his throat self-consciously)***:**

You know perfectly well that after sundown, especially on the Passover, nobody conducts business. Especially not in our pious religious community. That is strictly forbidden. I went there merely to maintain order and lend a sense of decorum among my colleagues.

SCRIBE:

So you ***were*** there!

CAIAPHAS *(reluctantly)***:**

Well, yes. But only because of the seriousness of the charges against this Man, Jesus.

SCRIBE:

What were the charges?

CAIAPHAS:

Blasphemy. Claiming to be equal to, and one with God.

SCRIBE:

That's *all*?

CAIAPHAS:

By law, that's more than enough to justify ordering his death.

SCRIBE:

But who *is* this Jesus?

CAIAPHAS:

From what we can ascertain, he is an itinerant preacher from a dirt-poor region of Galilee. He was raised in the home of a carpenter, and rumor has it that this Jesus was conceived out of wedlock. *(scoffing laugh)* Most people we interviewed said his mother is a pious woman. But that's doubtful, judging by the troublemaker she raised.

SCRIBE:

What kind of trouble?

CAIAPHAS:

Everywhere he went, he stirred up trouble. People flocked to his meetings by the droves. They held large meetings in the desert, away from the eyes and ears of the Romans. We sent some of our religious leaders to keep an eye on him. You know what a high stake we have in protecting the Israelis from further persecution by the Romans! We had to stop him before things got out of hand.

SCRIBE:

Did he preach the overthrow of our Roman rulers?

CAIAPHAS:

Oh, no, He was far too clever to do that in open air meetings. He seemed to talk in some kind of a code—parables. But it was very apparent to those in our ranks who infiltrated his meetings that many of His followers regarded Him as the Messiah.

SCRIBE *(excited, as if welcoming the idea)***:**

Really? What made his followers believe that?

CAIAPHAS:

The Messianic hope is all that sustains the people's faith. Generation after generation, since the period of Captivity, we have held out hope to the people that the Messiah will come and reestablish the Kingdom of David to our land. It's a useful ploy and helps most of our people bear up under the hardships imposed by our oppressors. *(sighs)* We have enjoyed very little self-governance since the Persians and Assyrians led our people into captivity.

SCRIBE:

But God has promised to send us a Messiah?

CAIAPHAS:

That is one way of interpreting the Scripture. Myself, I see my role as a peacemaker. We Jews are not a free people, so it's my job to keep the Roman governor Pilate and his bully boys from any excessive show of force against our countrymen. At whatever cost, we must preserve our history and our traditions as God's people. Jerusalem must remain uncorrupted by pagan influences, and that is best done, in my view, by involving the religious establishment in the political process. For you see, from top to bottom, we priests are the glue that holds everything together . . . past, present *and* future.

SCRIBE:

Sounds like you have a huge responsibility, and a large role to play in keeping the peace.

CAIAPHAS:

I take my responsibility very seriously.

SCRIBE:

So, getting back to this Jesus. This One whom some people looked to as the Messiah. Why was He considered so dangerous?

CAIAPHAS:

His popularity among the common folk had grown to the point where we feared an uprising. Mind you, there have been other "Messiahs" who've tried to shake the yoke of Rome.

No, no. We couldn't ignore this Jesus. He—well, he was different. Very tricky fellow. When we attempted to get Him to speak out against the heavy taxes imposed by the Romans, He said, "Render unto Caesar what is Caesar's, and unto God what belongs to Him." He even went so far as to tell one of his fishermen friends to throw out a line and haul in a fish that had swallowed a coin. He paid His tax in this bizarre fashion, just to flaunt His amusement with us for asking such a question. Why, He turned the whole thing into a *joke*! Can you imagine?

And . . . and this same Jesus consorted with men who smelled of fish and had dirt under their fingernails. All the outcasts and nobodies flocked to hear Him. He appealed to the disenfranchised and the dregs of society. Of *course* He was dangerous!

SCRIBE:

His followers don't sound like they had enough money to help him rise to power.

CAIAPHAS:

He made a mockery of power and money. He overturned the money changers in the temple and threw them out, while His followers cheered. He had an answer for every religious question raised. Oh, He had a quick wit and a smart mouth, that One! No matter what question was put to Him, He always turned it around so that *we* looked bad!

SCRIBE:

I remember He spoke once in obscure terms about living water, which I assumed was a criticism of our public wells.

CAIAPHAS:

You see: Exactly the kind of insult I would expect from this upstart.

SCRIBE:

So you had him arrested, interrogated and flogged. And then crucified.

CAIAPHAS:

(trying to preserve his image as a reasonable man)

I wouldn't put it quite that way. I had done my best to dismiss his actions as those of a madman, especially after rumors came to us from Bethany that he was being credited with raising a man named Lazarus from the dead. Such poppycock!

SCRIBE *(making note on tablet)***:**

Did you check out the story?

CAIAPHAS:

Of course not! We had enough information from our spies to know it was time to shut down his operation. The danger of an uprising was now imminent, and we couldn't risk a blood bath of retaliation from the Romans.

SCRIBE:

So you and the Sanhedrin were forced to act?

CAIAPHAS:

Absolutely. We were under great pressure to keep Rome happy. So you can see why it was so important for Jesus to be sacrificed, one life for the lives of an entire nation.

SCRIBE:

Just one more question: What if Jesus *were* the Messiah?

CAIAPHAS *(smirking)***:**

Well, that's something we'll never know, isn't it? What matters is that I acted in time to preserve the religious establishment, which is the very backbone of our social and economic strength.

SCRIBE:

Yes, but didn't it bother you, just a little—

CAIAPHAS *(losing temper)***:**

Now listen to me, Scribe, and listen well: ***I*** was in control! I had to decide quickly or relinquish power to that pompous, potbellied potentate Pilate! *(practically frothing at the mouth)* What did you expect? Do you honestly think I could afford to look weak? It took me *years* to get to where I am in life! I rose to leadership on my own, and nobody—especially not some carpenter's son from Nazareth—was going to stop me!

SCRIBE *(slow to understand)***:**

Sounds like you had a difficult choice to make.

CAIAPHAS:

Yes, and I did the right thing! *(totally exasperated)* Now get out of here before I have you hauled up on charges for questioning my authority!

*[**SCRIBE** EXITS in opposite direction from **CAIAPHAS**.]*

THE GAMBLER

[Soldier ENTERS, rattling dice in a cup]

All right, my friends, place your bets. Who's going to win that preacher man Jesus' cloak? A fine piece of goods it is, worth a week's wages in the marketplace.

[Throws his dice.] Snake eyes!

Sorry to disappoint you, but I'm a hard man to beat. Around here, I'm known as the Gambling Man. It's in my blood. Stronger than wine, without giving me the blind staggers. *(cynical laugh)* Mustn't lose control. A soldier never lets his job get to him.

So I don't drink. I gamble.

[Points into audience] Hey, you! Yeah, you! You who look down your nose at me, what makes you think my weakness is any worse than yours? Huh?

But since it bothers you, let me tell you why I gamble.

Playing the odds takes my mind off my work. Keeps me from letting it get to me. Reminds me that we're all up for grabs. Nothing in life is certain.

Being a soldier is a lonely, dirty job. The hours are long, the pay is often a year late in coming, and the food we get barely keeps a body alive. So I got me a sideline. I run a little business on the side, selling black market goods, used clothing, like this fine robe. *[holds up robe, offering it]* Any takers?

[Admires robe.] This Jesus must have some rich friends!

[Puts down the robe, returns to explaining himself.]

I like gambling. Besides helping me survive the messier aspects of my work, it pays good. So I'm a betting fool. That's how I get my kicks. Betting on fate. Betting on which fly caught in a spider's web is going to get eaten first by the spider! Or betting which of these crummy prisoners is gonna die first. Things like that. I enjoy my little hobby. It makes the time pass, and keeps me from thinking too deep.

Throwing dice is like life, all a matter of chance.

Being a soldier in the Roman Army, I never know where fate will take me, or if I'll live long enough to see my family again. Most of us won't. If dysentery or cholera doesn't kill us, we'll likely get run through by a rusty sword, right? Life in the Army leaves a lot to be desired.

In my case, I didn't enlist. What? Do you think I'm stupid? No way!

I was taken by force aboard a slave galley bound for Egypt.

They gave me two choices: Fight for Caesar, or get tossed overboard.

How do you like them odds? Life, or death. Flip of the coin.

Being a poor swimmer, I chose to serve at the Emperor's pleasure.

Eventually I wound up in Capernaum as part of the Praetorium Guard.

Surprised? Yeah, thought you would be. But I figured as long as fate made me a soldier, I'd better learn to excel in combat and work my way up through the ranks.

Maybe if I keep my wits about me, I'll get promoted to Centurion, like Marcus, my superior officer. Now, he's a piece of work, let me tell you.

While Marcus was stationed in a dusty outpost in Capernaum, he married one of the local babes. Even had a few kids. Big mistake, if you ask me, but then, I'm not crazy about commitment. Life's too unpredictable. Who wants to get tied up in anything too serious?

Well, anyway, Marcus got along great with the local people in Capernaum. His little wife attended synagogue, and before long, Marcus is going, too. He really digs this "God" stuff, y'know?

I used to ask him, "Which God?" but all I got back was a vague answer.

"The one true God," he said. Huh! Give me a break! I long ago quit believing any of the gods were looking out for me. Me, ***I*** look out for

Numero Uno. That's Number One, in case you wonder. Me, the one and only. *(bows)*

But I guess Marcus was hoping to stay put. And why not? Being a centurion, he had a nice house. Servants. He made friends with everyone, the Jewish elders, the townspeople. Things were going great for Marcus. I have to admit I was a little jealous.

To get to where he was, I figured I had to work even harder.

So when this guy here *(gestures toward the cross)*, this Rabbi Jesus, started preaching in the area, I started nosing around and keeping tabs on who went to His open air meetings. One of our jobs was keeping an eye out for trouble makers. Jesus sure drew a crowd, let me tell you!

He started to attract attention when He preached in the synagogue in Nazareth. Whatever his sermon topic was that day, He sure upset the local rabbi. Nearly got himself thrown off a cliff.! Marcus had to send a squadron of soldiers to Nazareth to restore order.

Jesus moved on to Capernaum, and people continued to follow him in droves.

People came from miles around. Sometimes I counted four, maybe five thousand people at one of his meetings. Starving people, social outcasts, sick people carried on stretchers. They dogged Jesus' steps wherever He went.

What was the big attraction? He was a healer, and He talked about the "kingdom of God," whatever that is. To me, it sounded like a bunch of hogwash. Being nice to people who hate you . . . where does that get you?

I never could make sense out of His stories. But the crowds kept growing. They couldn't seem to get enough of His teaching!

Some of us figured maybe Jesus was talking in some kind of secret code to incite a revolt. Now I remember: He spoke in *parables!* Only I never could prove he was talking treason. I did my best, but I failed.

Meanwhile Jesus kept healing people, casting out demons—Hey, let me tell you the time He visited this weird guy who lived in a graveyard! If I hadn't seen this wild man sitting calmly at Jesus' feet, I never would have believed it! The guy was cured!

Let me tell ya, this guy was one of the scariest, out-of-control freaks in the region. And there he was, wearing clothes and talking just like you or me.

Of course, there were a lot of angry pig farmers, but hey, who cares? Although I gotta admit I could have made a fortune selling dead pigs to the Syrians, if I coulda gotten to the carcasses in time. But that's another story, another lost opportunity.

So where was I? Oh, yeah. I was chasing Jesus around, keeping tabs on Him. He preached in all the little towns, and often came to Capernaum, where He had many friends.

On one such occasion, Marcus's servant was ill and not expected to live. He'd made himself really valuable to Marcus as a translator and securing supplies for the garrison. We all relied heavily on his knowledge of local customs and officials.

Marcus was already strongly influenced by the Jewish religion, so when he heard that Jesus was in town, he sent several men to ask Jesus to come and heal his servant. They reminded Jesus what an upstanding man the Centurion was, and how he'd helped build the Jewish synagogue. Of course, Jesus never could say "No," and so He went right away.

But before Jesus got there, the Centurion sent word, "Lord, don't trouble yourself. I don't deserve to have you come under my roof. That is why I didn't feel worthy to come to you. Just say the word, and my servant will be healed. For I myself am a man under authority, with soldiers under me. I tell this one, 'Go,' and he goes, and that one, 'Come,' and he comes. I say to my servant, 'Do this,' and he does it."

Well, I stood there, my mouth hanging open! Marcus figured Jesus could just say, "Be healed," without even seeing his servant or laying hands on him, and the servant would be healed? ***Unbelievable!***

Even Jesus was surprised, but as it turned out, for a different reason. He turned to the people following him through the street and said, "I tell you, I have not found such great faith, even in Israel."

So He went on His way. When the Jewish elders returned to Marcus's house, they found his servant perfectly well. Pretty amazing, wouldn't you say?

Me, I was dumbfounded. I don't know where this Jesus got His power, but He's like nobody else I ever met, or heard of.

No wonder the people wanted to make Him their King.

Well, you can see where that got Him! *[Again he gestures to the cross.]*

Of course, I never heard Him actually agree to such an idea, but when people in an occupied country start talking crazy, it's inevitable that the authorities had to step in.

Anyway Jesus was still preaching in the hills and from the back of a fisherman's boat, when our forces were transferred to Jerusalem. I tell you, Marcus was torn up bad. Broke down and cried. Didn't I warn him not to get too sappy about the wife and kids?

When you serve in Caesar's Army, you gotta be ready to pick up and move at a moment's notice. I say a man in the military is better off not getting too attached emotionally—bound to suffer disappointment when he has to move on. Like I was saying, army life leaves something to be desired. Maybe when I get me enough money, I'll find a place on the coast of Italy and settle down. Who knows?

Meanwhile I'm just a soldier stationed in a country full of religious nuts. They crucify a man for being too honest. For kicking thieves out of the temple.

So how do I feel about what's going on right now?

Dumb question! What do you expect me to say? Do you think I like crucifixion? Truth is, it's a dirty business.

Besides, there are faster, more merciful ways to kill a man.

Personally, if I had my choice, I'd use the garrotte, or beheading.

But I'm not the one in charge. I don't think up ways to kill.

I just follow orders.

I don't think *any* of us, including my commander, would be out here in this wind and heat and dust, listening to the screams of agony and trying to keep the crowd under control, if we weren't under orders.

Marcus has been really torn up by Jesus' crucifixion. He idolized Jesus.

Me, I try not to take it too personal. Still I can see Marcus's point: It's a rotten way to reward a Friend for healing your servant.

Being a loyal soldier, and seeing how broken up Marcus is, naturally I volunteered to do the scourging. *[Becomes defensive and starts to lose his composure.]* Somebody had to do it! I'm no sadist. Yeah, I made fun and knocked Him around a bit. I'm not proud of it. Sometimes a man does things to keep from showing his true feelings.

It's my job, man! Do you think I enjoyed nailing them spikes? Do you?

Well, you're wrong! Crucifixion makes no sense to me. Nobody deserves such torture. I just did what I had to do, and then I—

Hey, if you'd been there, you'd understand where I'm coming from. It was nothing personal. I had to block out what was going on around me. This Jesus is a hard Person to ignore, let me tell you!

I-I heard Him talking about forgiveness, and saying goodbye to his mother. I never got to say goodbye to *my* mother! I was just herded onto a ship.

How do you think I felt, listening to Him struggle to breathe? And . . . when He cried through parched lips, "I thirst," who do you think ran to give him the sponge dipped in wine vinegar?

Me, that's who! I wanted it over! I didn't know how much more pain He or I could endure—

When He died, a great earthquake rocked the ground, splitting great boulders and knocking down buildings as far as the eye could see. People screamed and fled for their lives.

But not me. My orders were to guard the body of Jesus and the other two. So I swallowed my fear and my hatred of a system that makes life cheap! I stood at my post, the ground shaking beneath my boots.

Hey, man, I'm not afraid! It—it was just the ground shaking.

Ain't nothing supernatural going on, I swear! And I pretend I don't hear Marcus shout, "Truly, this man was the Son of God!"

"Shut up, man!" I yell at him. But he's down on his knees now, asking forgiveness of a dead man.

For that bit of reckless heresy, Marcus could lose his post. Possibly give up his life. For we are sworn to give our full allegiance to Caesar, not praise the bloody corpse of a common carpenter-turned-preacher!

Whatever I think of Jesus, I'm keeping it to myself!

Now, leave me be! Go on, get outa here! *(gestures dismissively)* I got better things to do than explain myself to curiosity seekers.

[Rattles the dice; resumes his brashness.] I'm the gambling man. And if gambling's a vice, that's fine by me. It's all I got to see me through the dirty business we've engaged in here today. Helps dull the hurt and the shame.

[His voice breaks.] Oh, Jesus, help me . . . forget.

OFFSTAGE VOICE:

"Father, forgive them, for they don't know what they do."

[Or use another related Scripture to lead into a Lenten message.]

Joseph of Arimathea, Reporting to Pontius Pilate

PONTIUS PILATE *(shaking hands)*:

I appreciate you coming to share what happened out there today, Joseph. It wouldn't look good for me to be present. Some might think I was having second thoughts about ordering His execution.

JOSEPH:

Yes, I realize your position is a difficult one.

PONTIUS PILATE *(cynical smile)*:

A juggling act, you mean. It's impossible to please everyone. I do my best to keep the peace, but—. *(shrugs)*—So tell me what transpired.

JOSEPH:

It was heartbreaking to me personally. As you know, I voted against the Council's decision to have Jesus crucified. With no evidence of wrongdoing, the leaders had two men testify. Both known liars and bribe takers. No valid charge could be found for bringing Him before the religious Council.

PONTIUS PILATE:

I've been here long enough to absorb much that is good in your culture, but for the life of me, I can't understand how the Council can quote, "Thou shalt not kill," and then in the next breath condemn a man to death for making a few rash claims that are patently absurd!

This Jesus told me flat out—in the most disarming and direct way imaginable!—"My kingdom is not of this world. If it were, my followers would fight to prevent my arrest." I tell you, Joseph, Jesus showed no sign of wanting to overthrow the Roman government. He made no threats. When I asked if He was a king, He confirmed it, saying, "You are right in saying I am a king. For this reason I was born, and for this cause, I came to testify to the truth."

JOSEPH:

What did you conclude from such a statement?

PONTIUS PILATE:

I concluded that He was a harmless Jewish rabbi, totally lacking in personal ambition. Certainly He was no threat to Rome, or to anyone else, for that matter. *(rubs chin, considering)* Although . . . I must admit His directness of manner was a bit disconcerting. "What is Truth?" I asked Him. *(low cynical laugh)*

JOSEPH *(gently)*:

Did He tell you?

PONTIUS PILATE:

No, of course not. But does it matter? *(sighs)* Truth has a way of changing to suit the situation. I tried to dissuade the Council, but they were out for blood. They insisted that Jesus was too great a threat. And so they turned to me to do their dirty work.

JOSEPH:

I noticed what you posted as His crime—above His cross?—"Jesus of Nazareth—King of the Jews."

PONTIUS PILATE:

Oh, that. *(chuckles)* I was just getting back at old Caiaphas.

JOSEPH:

I wondered why you ordered it to read, "King of the Jews." It was quite a slap in the face to many of my colleagues.

PONTIUS PILATE:

And you, Joseph? Were you offended?

JOSEPH:

You worry too much about giving offense. You need to let your honest feelings come out more.

PONTIUS PILATE:

Bah! I have no honesty left in me. I lost whatever sense of honor and decency I had years ago. Comes with the job.

JOSEPH *(touches Pilate on the arm)***:**

I see a lot of good in you, my friend.

PONTIUS PILATE *(shrugs)***:**

Remember all the uproar and the crowd insisting that I release Barrabas, a notorious serial killer? I tell you, Joseph, there was no justice done this day! I am still sick to my stomach with disgust.

The whole city was preparing to celebrate the Passover, when their god Yahweh showed great mercy to the entire nation of Israel. So what happens?

Instead of releasing an innocent Man, I found myself caving in and granting the crowd's wish. I let a vile murderer go free!

And this Jesus—a more decent, likable fellow I've never met—a Man who had done no wrong, I might add—was put to death in the place of the vilest offender! I tell you, Joseph, after today I entertain no delusions about the kind of a man I am!

JOSEPH:

We are all sinners. Prone to do things we're ashamed of.

PONTIUS PILATE:

I'm a craven coward!

JOSEPH:

I, too. I feel so helpless. I wanted to find some loophole in the Mosaic Law and save Jesus. He was, as you said, a righteous Man. Pilate, I wish you could have been there when He was crucified.

PONTIUS PILATE:

You know why I couldn't show my face! As unpopular as I am, there's no doubt in my mind there would have been an attempt on my life.

JOSEPH:

Yes, but if you *had* been there, you might not be so full of self-hatred now. Jesus spoke of forgiveness and love. I'm sure He understood your dilemma.

PONTIUS PILATE:

If you say so. But the fact remains that He's dead now. A poor Teacher with only the clothes on His back.

JOSEPH:

Not even that. They were all gambled away. Even his cloak.

PONTIUS PILATE:

Destined for a pauper's grave, then.

JOSEPH:

Actually, that is the real reason I came to see you.

PONTIUS PILATE:

What? *[Joseph hesitates, and Pilate grows impatient.]* The Man's dead, Joseph. I made a big mistake. Well? Speak up, man! What else is there to say?

JOSEPH:

I hoped, in keeping with the nature of His "crime," *(slight smile in voice)* Well, I'd like to bury Him in my own tomb, Pontius.

PONTIUS PILATE *(shocked)***:**

Are you serious? You've spent a fortune building that tomb! Don't you think you're getting a little carried away with emotion? I mean, if it were me—

JOSEPH:

Jesus was a real friend to me. I've never spoken openly about it before, but Jesus helped me deal with some tough personal issues. And now I feel the least I can do for Him is provide Him with a burial place that does Him honor.

PONTIUS PILATE *(amused)***:**

A tomb worth a king's ransom for the "King of the Jews," eh?

JOSEPH:

Something like that. Maybe He's not "King of the Jews," but in my heart, I'll always think of Him as my mentor. Jesus changed my life, made a new man of me.

PONTIUS PILATE:

Then, go, my friend, and bury this crucified "Mentor" of yours. Perhaps in some small measure that will ease your grief. *[Quickly scribbles an Order and hands it to Joseph.]*

JOSEPH:

Thanks, Pontius. I am much in your debt.

PONTIUS PILATE:

(shakes hands with a larcenous smile)

You know me, Joseph. I always find a way to call in my debts! *(waves hand dismissively)* Now go! I have other business to attend, and a party tonight.

[As JOSEPH exits, PILATE looks out the window, then turns to call out to JOSEPH:]

Hurry, Joseph! The sky is dark, and the wind's screaming around the palace walls like the souls of the lost.

[Drops head into hands; gives way to a moment of personal grief.]

Oh, Jesus, forgive . . .

[After a slight pause, he EXITS, head bowed.]

Note: According to the *Encyclopaedia Britannica*, legend has it that Joseph of Arimathea later traveled as a missionary to Gastonbury, in what is now Great Britain. Readers of church history may wish to research the subject further.

John Mark, Writer of One of the Gospels

JOHN MARK:

I must admit that the circumstances surrounding Jesus' arrest in the Garden were, for me, more than a little embarrassing. I can still recall my mother's shock when I got home, and the questioning look in her eyes.

How did I happen to be there in the first place? Perhaps you wonder how is it that I left the scene stark naked? What really happened out there?

To answer these and other more crucial questions, it is necessary to retrace our steps back to earlier that evening. Although not among Jesus' inner circle of disciples, I was a follower. True, I was quite young, but His teachings, and especially His understanding heart, drew me as a teenager. I had been raised by strict, though loving parents. From a small boy, I knew the teachings of the Talmud and our nation's history. But I never was very interested in my heritage until Jesus came to town.

I first heard Him open the Scriptures to my friends and me after a slight altercation in the marketplace. My friends and I were stuffing melons under our tunics. I had sufficient money in my pocket to pay for the melons, but before I could, the vendor became upset. I admit we'd had a bit too much wine and our judgment was impaired, but we really meant no serious harm. Anyway, we were laughing and waddling around like pregnant women, when suddenly, this pair of really strong arms reached out and gathered us into a giant bear hug.

"What are you boys up to?" He asked in a deep voice.

"N-nothing," I stammered, as I looked up into the warmest pair of brown eyes, smiling and full of good humor. Right away I knew I had found a Friend.

Jesus was with a group of men as travel worn as He was. They had just bought food for their noon meal. When He invited me and my friends to join them—provided we made our peace with the vendor—of course, I paid her right away and offered my profuse apologies.

We wandered along through the crowd of shoppers, and here and there, He stopped to speak to people. He could strike up a friendship with anyone! Even people He had never met before were instantly taken with Him. Soon my friends and I were part of an ever increasing circle of friends moving through the streets.

It wasn't quite noon, and I remember feeling this indescribable joy, like a great happiness welling up inside. Even when my sister married and we feasted for days, I never felt like this! Being near Jesus made me feel important, like I was in the presence of a king. Or Messiah perhaps? That's what many people were saying about Him.

But let's move ahead to the night of His arrest.

I had hung around to help serve the Passover meal. Mostly women did such tasks, but I was willing to peel vegetables and turn the spit on the roasting lamb, just to be near Jesus. That night started out as a celebration, but Jesus' mood grew more serious as the meal came to a close. He talked about dying. Of being betrayed and going away to prepare a place for His friends. Busy as I was, I only caught snatches of the conversation, but what I heard made me worry. I decided to follow Jesus when He left the party.

Peter, James and John went with Him to the Garden of Gethsemane. I remember the moonlight on the hillside, and the spooky shadows among the olive trees. His friends fell asleep, so I figured Jesus must be safe. After all, what could happen to Him so late at night? Plus He was praying.

So I left without disturbing Him.

I went home to bed. Only I couldn't sleep. Things Jesus had said at the Passover feast kept going through my mind. Who was going to betray Him, I wondered. When was all this supposed to happen? What did He mean He had to die? If He were truly the Messiah, as many thought, wasn't He supposed to lead a great army against the Romans, defeat them, and reign as King?

As the night wore on, I grew more and more restless. Jesus was my Friend. I had pretty much made up my mind that I must not have heard Him right. After all, I was in and out of the Upper Room all night, carrying platters, bringing more wine—

[SOUND EFFECT: Loud Knock]

Then came a knock at my father's door. I sat bolt upright in bed. Who could it be at this hour? I heard the muffled voices of my father and a neighbor, and then I knew: A group of soldiers had just passed our house in the dead of night. They were on their way to arrest Jesus in the Garden.

I jumped out of bed. I hadn't a stitch of clothes on me. Quickly I threw a tunic over my head. I had to warn Jesus! There was still time for Him to escape, if I hurried.

I ran as never before. My heart was racing.

My feet barely hit the ground. *(Simulates arms pumping.)*

Oh, please, God! Don't let Jesus still be there when the soldiers come!

I ran faster still, but it was too late.

My Master and Friend was being bound, hands behind His back.

Peter and James and John just stood there, frozen with fear.

"Don't just stand there! *Do* something!" I cried. I ran toward them, the desert wind cold against my legs. "Run, Jesus! Save yourself."

Desperate now for my Friend, I bumped into the soldier standing beside Jesus. Perhaps if I created a distraction—

But Jesus shook His head. "This isn't your fight, Mark."

"But I want to help! . . . I-I love you!"

"I know, lad. Now go home," He said in a gentle voice.

A soldier grabbed me by the back of my tunic.

In a panic, I ducked—and left him holding my tunic.

Stark naked, I ran, the wind howling around me, as I sought the safety of my parents' home. My heart was breaking. Was there nothing I could do to save my Friend?

As it turned out, the answer was No. I could do nothing, for Jesus had to face death. He was destined to die as a common criminal, taking my place and yours on that Cross. He died to free us from the oppression of sin and fears that grip us. He came to set us free!

But I am also happy to report: His death was not the end of the story.

Jesus rose again and appeared to all His disciples. Hundreds of us gathered on the Mount of Olives to witness His ascension to the Father many days after His resurrection. I saw Him with my own eyes.

My friends, He is alive!

He will always be my Friend—and yours, if you'll let Him.

He sends His Spirit to help us each day.

Yes, my friends, Jesus is alive! *[Places his fist over his heart.]*

In our hearts for all time!

Mary the Mother of Jesus, Coming from the Scene of His Death

[Reporter is talking to people as they leave the scene of the Execution of Jesus. He sticks a microphone in the face of a woman hurrying along, weeping, her head covered.]

REPORTER:

You were there at the foot of the Cross. *(astonished)* Why, it's Jesus' mother! *(aside to audience)* What a scoop for me!

Tell me, Mary, mother of Jesus, what precisely went through your mind, as you watched your Son being put to death as a common criminal?

MARY *(patiently)***:**

What do you expect? I'm still in shock.

I keep asking myself, How could this have happened? I know these are violent times, but I never expected my Son—my perfect Son, who never lied, or cheated, or did anything but good to His fellow man—would be arrested, falsely accused, and put through the mockery of a trial—held in secret and at midnight!—And then they nailed Him to that terrible cross.

[Shakes her head and holds onto a sturdy prop to steady her.]

REPORTER *(a trifle smug)*:

I suppose it's hard for a mother to be objective about her son. Obviously He must have committed *some* crime, or they wouldn't have crucified Him.

MARY:

He was innocent, I tell you! Completely without sin.

If He was guilty of anything, it was of loving people too much and of making friends with sinners. He went out of his way to encourage and heal and lift up the downtrodden. He loved people from every walk of life.

Children occupied a special place in His heart. He loved to tell them stories. He cared about their problems and really paid attention to what they had to say.

REPORTER *(incredulous)*:

He liked brats? But they're noisy and dirty and disruptive!

MARY:

Jesus saw good in everyone. He could look right past the fake smiles and see the heartache, or the shame, or despair. He could make friends with just about anyone.

Even a corrupt politician like Zacchaeus, who robbed people blind.

And that Samaritan woman, whose life was full of scandal, and looked down on by everyone. She came upon Jesus at the well in the heat of the day, getting her water while everyone else was taking a siesta.

Jesus was a man's man. He loved to climb mountains and go fishing with other men.

And He could sure hold His own with the rabbis and smart folk, too, like that Nicodemus.

No, I tell you, no man ever walked this earth and loved people the way my Jesus did. He was something special, I tell you . . . *(begins to think back)* . . . from the very beginning..

REPORTER:

And yet he wound up dying the most torturous death imaginable . . . nailed to a cross and gasping for every breath. A long, drawn out torture, reserved for only the vilest, most terrible criminals.

MARY:

[No longer listening to the reporter, but thinking back]

I remember when the angel spoke to me out on the hills near Nazareth. Such an innocent I was in those days! And when the angel told me that God had chosen me—***me,*** an insignificant young nobody from a poor working class family—to be the mother of God's only Son—

I tell you, my heart nearly burst with rejoicing!

Like everyone else, I had heard the prophets' words, that the Messiah, the mighty Deliverer, would be born of a virgin, but I never dreamed it would be me.

(Looking up, reliving the past) "How can this be?" I asked.

To this day, I can't explain it.

But what none of us can understand with our finite mind, God brought to pass with no more effort than the formulation of a plan.

And, O, what a plan! I used to wonder why God chose me, instead of a princess to have His Son.

Joseph was crazy about our little baby! I was so blessed to have him at my side. He was wiser than I in so many ways. He said God sent His Son to a poor homeless couple to show the whole world that He wasn't standoffish, that he wanted to bless everyone.

God wanted His Son to be a Friend to poor folk, who had no fit shelter from the storms of life, so that they would let Him be their strong Defender against the injustices of this world.

And so for over thirty years I was privileged to witness God in the flesh, revealing Himself to us in all the ordinary events of life.

Jesus, the visible expression of the invisible God!

I still marvel that such a thing could have come to pass.

And yet now my heart is heavy, and I weep for the Son who is no more. After what took place today—*(shudders)*—I feel as if my heart has been torn in two. I can barely find the strength or the desire to go on without Him.

He was my life, my joy! My baby! O how I loved my Jesus!

Oh, the pain He suffered on that cross—! How could such an injustice be done to the sinless Son of the most high God? The Chosen One of Israel?

I know He was sent by His heavenly Father to save our people from bondage, but they have rejected Him and left His body covered with blood and sweat and flies.

What is wrong with people? How can they despise the truth and embrace such evil?

REPORTER:

Maybe God made a mistake? Did He, do you think?

MARY:

You mean, Did He really turn His back on His Son—and mine—when He cried out, "My God, my God, why have you forsaken me?"

Oh, sir, did you even once stop to consider—Where was God when all the sin and hatred and disgrace piled on my Son was so dark and filthy and foul that even the sun refused to shine through at noonday?

Did you ever wonder about that? I did!

It breaks my heart to think of my Jesus suffering in darkness . . . refusing even then to stop loving us . . . still praying . . . while He died on our behalf.

But was He really alone? Ask yourself that!

Jesus may have felt abandoned and cut off from His Heavenly Father, but if I, Jesus' mother, could not stop loving Him, even when He became sin Who knew no sin, I know a perfect and righteous God could not stop loving Him either. No, especially not then. At His darkest hour, God was there.

REPORTER:

Why would anyone bear such pain and still pray for His enemies? Why?

MARY:

Love. I have no other answer to that burning question. But all the "why?" questions in the world can't change the fact that my Son is dead, slaughtered. The sinless sacrificial Lamb, pure and unblemished.

His blood was shed for you and me and all those poor, miserable creatures who made sport, while He prayed for God to forgive their sins.

Jesus did it—for ***us***! Not because He was guilty, or deserved to die. He did it out of ***love*** for a world of lost, confused sinners like you and me.

REPORTER:

You make it sound as if we're ***all*** sinners, capable of great evil.

MARY:

Oh, sir, has nothing sunk in, after what happened here today?

Or taught you anything about human nature?

REPORTER *(sighs)***:**

It ***was*** pretty rough out there today, I admit. A most unfortunate death. A bad break for Jesus. But who can stop a lynch mob?

Still, I can understand how you as His mother would be upset.

But lots of injustices occur in this world. Lots of us lose a loved one. But if God really cared, or was listening, ***why*** is there so much misery in the world?

MARY:

(forgets her own grief; regards him with pity)

In other words, why did God allow this to happen?

Why does He allow any of us to suffer or experience tragic loss?

Because the Almighty Father is all wise. That's why He became flesh and blood and dwelt among us. Because He ***loves*** us!

And today is not the end, believe me.

Jesus has conquered every other enemy of mankind, and you may be sure He will conquer death as well.

Of course, I never expected things to turn out the way they did, but I do know that God is faithful. He keeps His promises. Nothing is too hard for Him.

And I also know that we're going to get past this loss through fellowship with Jesus in His sufferings.

He understands our pain! He knows what we're going through, every moment of every day! Because He has gone through so much—for ***us!***—He will never leave us comfortless.

Someday I will see Jesus again, face to face, with all the shekinah glory of God's angels shining down on us. I can trust God, no matter what!

His counsel is too high for me to attain. *My* understanding is limited, whereas God is all powerful, all wise. He is "a very present help in times of trouble."

No plan of His will ever fail. I have His word on it!

What better proof of God's power and love do I need, than the miracle that made it possible for me to conceive and bring into this world ***Jesus***, the only begotten Son of God?

He was my son, too. He was my Jesus. And my Savior.

(Raises her hands to the heavens) O, may the God of Abraham, Isaac and Jacob, the God who created the miracle of life in my womb so long ago, raise up Jesus to reign on high forever!

Even now, my soul doth magnify the Lord and rejoice!

(Takes hold of the reporter's arm.) Come, sir, let me show you where they have laid His body.

[EXEUNT together.]

NICODEMUS

For a long time I was known as "The Secret Disciple." In fact, if the truth were known, I suspect many of you present here today feel critical because I didn't come right out and declare myself as a follower of Jesus of Nazareth.

But I wonder how many of you would still condemn me for a coward, if you had lived in such troubled times? Certainly Jesus never uttered a word of condemnation. He understood my hesitation. At no time did He demand that I make a public stand.

He was more concerned about the *condition* of my soul than He was in numbers. What an amazing Man! From the beginning, He was responsive to my needs and most respectful of my desire for anonymity.

I remember our first meeting in secret. I had sent a message through a mutual acquaintance. Now, I admit some of my colleagues had put me up to it. They had a list of questions for me to put to Jesus, and their motives for asking were anything but pure.

But I was willing enough to meet this man Jesus. His fame had spread far and wide. He preached to hundreds—some say thousands—on the hillsides outside the towns, from the northernmost rural communities of Israel to the outskirts of Jerusalem. Word of miraculous healings also had reached the ears of the Council.

But when rumors that He was the Messiah, and that He claimed a personal relationship with Yahweh reached us, we grew alarmed. The potential threat this Man posed, if He amassed a great army of followers and went against the Romans, could only bring more bloodshed and misery to our tiny nation.

At this point, Caiaphas and those of us on the Council felt we had to get involved. We could no longer ignore the impact Jesus was having on the population.

And so we met, late one night.

He was nothing like what I had expected. There wasn't a militant bone in his body. He spoke not of war or political causes, but about living water and being born again.

He showed me such courtesy and patience, as I began my interrogation! He shook His head and smiled at my questions—well, actually, they were the Council's questions. He seemed saddened that I, a man who claimed to be spiritually enlightened, would waste an entire evening on such foolishness.

He asked me about my childhood and my family. How were my children? Did I love my wife? Did she love me? Was it love at first sight? When I explained that it was an arranged marriage, he asked, Was I happy? Did I ever long for more satisfying work? Had I found peace?

Throughout our conversation, He showed a total lack of interest in politics. He kept bringing the conversation back to my life, and what did *I* want, or feel was lacking.

When I finally ran out of questions that Caiaphas and the Sanhedrin wanted me to ask, He suddenly looked me straight in the eye and said, "You know what's missing, Nicodemus? You need to be born again."

Talk about being direct! Jesus had seen past all my evasiveness and urbane polish. The most astonishing shock wave swept over me. Here I was, one of the sharpest legal minds in the Council—educated, successful.

And then along comes this upstart country preacher from Galilee, telling me that I needed to be "born again."

Immediately I began to pose arguments, aimed at exposing His ignorance. Didn't He realize the illogic of such a remark? I was sure I would soon consign His high-sounding spiritual counsel to the dung heap. What this Man needed was a dose of humility!

Inside I was furious, but I held onto my temper outwardly. I was determined to remain calm and friendly; never give Him the upper hand. "How can a man be born again when he is old?" I asked. "Must he reenter his mother's womb a second time to be born again?"

Of course, we all know such a thing is impossible. Without coming right out, I hoped to annihilate this Jesus and put a stop to His radical teaching, once and for all.

But did Jesus pay any attention to my logic? Not at all! He merely smiled and said, "I tell you the truth, Nicodemus, no one can enter the Kingdom of God unless he is born of water and the Spirit. Flesh gives birth to flesh, but the Spirit gives life to our spirit. You should not be surprised at my saying you must be born again."

By now I was blubbering and stumbling over my words like a child. "B-but why do you bring it up to me?" I asked. "I'm a decent person, well thought of. Pretty well satisfied with my situation in life."

Jesus shook His head. "Are you truly convinced that a fine reputation and wealth are the best that life has to offer?"

"All right," I stalled. "Suppose I admit that occasionally I sense my emptiness inside and long for something more from life. I doubt seriously that being 'born again' is the solution."

Jesus looked me square in the eye. "The wind blows wherever it pleases. You hear its sound, but you cannot tell where it comes from, or where it is going. So it is with everyone born of the Spirit."

Then He explained to me from the Scriptures that what He was telling me should come as no surprise: "Just as Moses lifted up the serpent in the desert, so the Son of Man must be lifted up, that everyone who believes in Him may have eternal life."

Now I realize that he was describing the kind of death He would die, but at the time I was stunned by His knowledge of holy writ. In a flash, I realized that I was in the presence of the Promised One, spoken of by the prophets. All my attempts to trick Jesus and show Him up as a false teacher had led me to the Truth Incarnate. He was standing right before me!

The Deliverer. Son of the Most High God.

Yet His Kingdom was not of this world, I also recognized. Jesus was no fraud. He was all the average person in the street claimed He was, and more. So much more.

My defenses fell from me completely. As His hand came to rest briefly in benediction on my head, I was born of the Spirit.

From that time on, I was new inside. Life began to open up to me in exciting new ways. I examined my role as a husband and began to behave differently, to be more patient and supportive of my wife. I didn't take my position of authority so seriously. I listened to my colleagues—not just the words they spoke. I began to listen to the heart cry of my fellow man. I no longer walked through the streets preoccupied with myself. I began to see what was going on around me in an entirely new light.

I tell you, coming to know Jesus has opened my eyes and made a new man of me!

Now I became an advocate for Jesus in the Council. On more than one occasion, they had sent guards out to arrest Him, but each time they came back empty-handed. The chief priests and Pharisees were incensed, because even a few of the guards had fallen under the spell of Jesus' teachings.

Clearly things were coming to a crisis point.

Caiaphas and the high priests were concerned that the Romans would impose even greater sanctions and create even more hardship for the people. The common folk must cease to rally around Jesus, they decided. Any day now, we expected trouble from the Romans.

The Council began to convene almost daily. Whenever they were in session, I made a point of being there. Not to spy and report back to Jesus, mind you, for He cared nothing for how the politicians ran things.

I went to plead for a fair and impartial hearing.

I argued, "How can we condemn a man who has not violated the law?"

My words might as well have fallen on deaf ears.

Caiaphas was determined to get rid of Jesus. He felt it was better that one man die to save the nation, and thus avoid an uprising among the people, followed by a blood bath of retaliation by the occupying forces.

Nothing I said swayed the Council from their decision to arrest Jesus. They held a mock trial in the dead of night. I was not informed until the next morning, and by then, it was too late. Jesus had already been turned over to the Romans for execution.

By the time I made my way out the city gates to Golgotha, Jesus had already been crucified. He hung there between two notorious thieves, a public spectacle for all to see. The crowd threw garbage and mocked and cursed Him. This Man, who was a Friend to everyone He met, was spit upon and reviled.

I almost didn't recognize Him. His face and body had been severely beaten. Despite the cruelty and pain He endured, in His darkest hour Jesus spoke only words of love and compassion and forgiveness. My heart broke, and I wept to see my Friend and spiritual mentor suffer so terribly.

He once told me, "For God so loved the world that He gave His one and only Son, that whoever believes in Him shall not perish but have eternal life."

Now at last I understood Jesus' mission: He had come to save me. Not an impersonal mob. He didn't die because of a faceless crowd of sinners. He died for me—and you—and for everyone of us here today!

He loves you! *(gestures to audience)* And you! He went to that cross for ***our*** sins.

He came as the sacrificial Lamb to rescue us all from the sure destruction of actions and words and attitudes that hurt and cut us off from family members and friends, and people whom we in our self-preoccupation have ignored. Jesus paid the penalty for us!

I tell you: All our vileness and small pettiness, all our selfishness and sin were nailed to that cross. That's how much He loves us!

I stood in numb shock, as the truth of His love for me sank in.

Passover was not some greasy feast to commemorate God's deliverance in the past. It is ***right now***, embodied in Jesus Himself! In the present.

I saw God's deliverance in the filthiest place I have ever stood—at the foot of Jesus' cross. To hear Him say, "Father, forgive them, for they don't know what they're doing," literally knocked me to my knees.

Several members of the Sanhedrin had come to the execution. They stayed just long enough to register their righteous scorn of rebel causes. They completely missed the point.

They, and others like themselves, claim to be on the side of peace. Jesus was too dangerous, they declared. His teachings were revolutionary and stirred up people's thinking. And, yes, they said, His death was a necessary thing to keep the status quo. Peace at any price best served the people.

After the priests and Sadducees left, Joseph of Arimathea arrived. A more even-handed man would be hard to find. He often served as liaison between Governor Pilate and the Jewish leaders. Like me, he was also a secret believer in Jesus.

The sky grew dark that fateful noon. The winds began to howl, and an earthquake sent the faint of heart fleeing from the scene! In truth, I was so grief-stricken that I couldn't have run for cover, even if I had wanted.

All I wanted was to stay with Jesus for as long as I could. I didn't want Him to die without friends there to pray for Him.

A few of us lingered at the foot of the cross. His mother, a few of his disciples, and, of course, the soldiers stayed to the bitter end. At last, Jesus cried out, "It is finished!"

I felt all the blood drain out of my head, and I fainted.

When I revived, Joseph was already taking down the body of Jesus from the cross. He passed among the soldiers, handing out coins. And then, tenderly, he gathered the lifeless body of Jesus into his arms.

"Nicodemus," he called. 'Come, give me a hand."

Unsteadily I got to my feet and helped to support Jesus' weight.

Weeping uncontrollably, Joseph kissed Jesus' face, wounds and all.

The soldiers looked embarrassed by this emotional display, but made no move to interfere.

"Don't worry. I have permission to bury my friend," Joseph gruffly told the Centurion. "I've already talked to Pilate."

With the soldiers' help, we carried Jesus to the tomb Joseph had designed for his own use on the Mount of Olives. Others came weeping to touch the body, but we sent them away, for night was rapidly approaching, and the Sabbath.

Joseph came well prepared. With heavy hearts, he and I bathed the body and wrapped it carefully, using a hundred pounds of spikenard, burial cloth and a linen shroud. The hour was late when we finished. Hurriedly, we placed Jesus' body in the tomb, and the soldiers sealed the entrance with a huge stone. And then, barely able to see through our tears, we stumbled home to our families and barred the door against the darkness.

Over the next three days, I wandered around in a fog of depression. I felt as if the sun would never shine again. All hope seemed gone, and the weight of the world weighed in on me, crushing my spirit.

But then Sunday at dawn, there came a knock at the door.

My wife, busy fixing breakfast, bless her, hurried through the darkened house. She opened the street door a crack.

After an urgent exchange of whispers, she called, "Nick! Come quick!"

Rubbing my eyes and smoothing my hair, I stumbled into the hall.

Two women stood there, beaming, with tears running down their faces.

The instant they saw me, they blurted out, "He is risen from the dead! He is alive!"

"Who?" I yawned, half-asleep.

"Jesus, that's who!" My wife jabbed me with her elbow. "The tomb is empty!"

GAMALIEL

I appreciate being asked for my perspective on the public life and ministry of the Nazarene, Jesus, and his trial and execution, neither of which do I condone.

Much of what happened was done in the heat of the moment. I myself felt that the Sanhedrin and the Pharisees allowed themselves to be unduly influenced by political pressures brought to bear upon our small nation by the Romans. Being ruled by a puppet king, Herod, many felt duty-bound to help keep the peace with Governor Pilate.

Imagine our dilemma! It wasn't easy to protect and practice our religion under the rule of such a crushing pagan power as Rome. Our job was to police our own citizens. You see, the real threat we faced was losing what little self-rule the citizens of Jerusalem still enjoyed. And so we focused on eliminating rabble rousers and revolutionary voices, who might stir up the population and bring the Roman Empire down on our tiny nation, destroying our homeland, deporting our families, and making slaves of us all. History has taught us well. Who would ever forget the horror of being held captive for seventy years by the Babylonians and Persian hordes?

These fears had a deep and abiding effect on every member of the Sanhedrin, scribes and Pharisees, I can assure you. Our nation has learned how to survive. During the Roman siege, we banded together for the purpose of survival.

Into this climate of fear, and looking, as we all were, for the Messiah, our Deliverer, came this wandering prophet, a laboring class fellow from a remote little town in the North. Religious rulers who heard this Jesus speak were frankly amazed by his ability to teach and to heal. Certainly there were few opportunities for education in Nazareth, where He came from, so one can only conclude that He was a *savant*, one of those people with a natural gift of expression and the ability to induce healing through the power of suggestion.

Jesus was quite the storyteller, oh, yes, he was!

Of course, one has to discount some of the more fantastic claims, that He raised people from the dead, cast out demons, and the like. I admit I was quite amazed when several lepers showed up at temple, claiming to have been healed. No sign of disease on them! Could be they had been faking all along. *(scratches his head)* But to what purpose? The priests' records indicated leprosy, but misdiagnosis might have accounted for some, though not all.

Clearly a good bath would have taken care of a bad skin rash. Certainly nobody would volunteer to be a leper. They couldn't even come close enough to the rest of the population to beg! So that argument washed out. They had to be telling the truth about their healing. That part seemed correct, but I sincerely questioned whether Jesus played an active role in their healing. After all, only God can heal. *(laughs)* As you can see, I am not prone to jumping to quick conclusions!

I questioned those who were brought to the Council, claiming that Jesus healed them. I couldn't shake their stories. Whatever happened to cure the leprosy, the blindness, or a crippled condition, such as paralysis, their testimonies seemed genuine enough.

I never will forget the woman with a bleeding disorder, who had been denied access to the rituals of her faith for several years. People from her synagogue finally concluded that she must have died. So imagine their surprise when she testified to being healed just by touching the hem of Jesus' garment!

As a scholar, I have come to value a calm, analytic approach to all questions, whether historic, medical, or spiritual in nature. After all these wild rumors about Jesus rising from the dead, a wave of panic swept through the Sanhedrin. The Pharisees were up in arms! How could they suppress this man Jesus' followers? Why, half the city saw Him crucified.

And yet His followers were going about, publicly declaring that He had overcome the last enemy any of us will face: Death. Strange rumors were running rampant, ridiculous claims about body snatchers and guards taking bribes, and Jesus meeting again with his followers.

Preposterous! I tell you, the Governor's office was in an uproar. Pilate had riot squads patrolling the streets, ready to squelch any uprising.

It was up to the Pharisees and the Sanhedrin to bury their differences and put an end to this nonsense. We had the ringleaders of this religious fanaticism arrested and brought into court to face charges. Common folk, they were, and utterly unimpressed by the fact that they were up against the best legal minds in the country!

The Council had just put James to death for speaking out against them, and now they had to decide the fate of his brother John, and the one they call the Big Fisherman. That Peter! He was a persuasive loudmouth and, in my opinion, one to watch carefully.

But the taking of life made me uncomfortable, especially after the underhanded way the Council had met to condemn Jesus to death in secret.

"Look," I told my colleagues, once I could make myself heard over the uproar within the Council chambers. "Time has a way of proving whether or not a particular event or personality will leave its mark on the face of history. It would be wrong for us to act in haste. After all, these are uneducated fishermen. We have seen exaggerated claims made by rebel leaders before, have we not? But in a very short time, support for their beliefs dissipated. The followers of this Man Jesus will doubtless lose interest, like all the others before them. ***But*** if this new teaching is from God, you won't be able to suppress it, for that would be a vain attempt to fight against God."

And so they ordered these two friends of Jesus to be flogged and released.

The rest is history.

About the Author

First published in her teens, **Barbara Dan** has enjoyed a variety of life experiences, including working as an actress, model, night club comedienne, singer/dancer, comedy writer, puppeteer, theatrical producer in Hollywood, screenwriter, publicist, fund-raiser, real estate saleswoman, hands-on builder of houses, escrow officer, co-teacher of couples' communications workshops with her Baptist minister husband, John Dan, as well as publisher, editor, adjunct college professor, and—by far her biggest joy and challenge—being mother to four now grown children and grandmother to five very lively grandchildren.

She credits the famed Hollywood Christian Group as a strong influence in her decision to become a Christian in 1958. She married her husband, then an actor, in 1959, and after he graduated from seminary in 1962, they served the Lord in a variety of Christian ministries in Utah, California, Illinois, and Las Vegas, Nevada, where he also directed a mental health center for the State of Nevada. During this time, she wrote the highly successful Christian screenplay ***Appointment*** and ghostwrote celebrity biographies for Cowboy Evangelist Leonard Eilers and Las Vegas Comedian Bernie Allen.

With family roots planted deep in New England history, Barbara is a voracious reader of history and has authored eleven novels. She enjoys quilting, gardening, oil painting, travel, tracking genealogies, and prowling around in old graveyards and musty museums doing research for her next historical novel.

Besides degrees in Theatre Arts and Advanced Accounting, she earned her M.A. in Humanities (main emphasis: literature) from California State University in 1988, but feels that life experience is the most valuable tool any writer brings to his or her work.

She is a member of both Women Writing the West and Western Writers of America, Inc.

For more information about Barbara Dan's books, visit www.barbaradan.com. Her eBooks are available in 31 countries via www.smashwords.com, eNook, Kindle, Apple, iPod, iPad, Diesel, Android, Baker & Taylor, etc. Her novels are available in print at amazon.com and distributors.